images of
ireland

"Teaing in the rain"

An Irish Portrait

people, land and spirit

Photography and Story by Ron Sanford

Published and Distributed by

John Hinde Ltd.

Dublin 18, Ireland

TEL. +353.1.294.1111

FAX +353.1.294.1071

Designed by Jerri Hemsworth

ISBN 1-901123-19-7

Whilst every care is taken in compiling this book,
no responsibility can be taken for errors or omissions.

images of ireland

An Irish Portrait

people, land and spirit

Contents

$\mathcal{M}$ost visitors depart the Emerald Isle with a good feeling about their stay. Even the Guinness starts to taste pretty good. "Struck" is the best way for me to describe my first Irish experience. It kind of happened without much in the way of my early participation. I was wrapped up, carried along, by a sense of kindness, and unquestioning consideration, that is unique among other nationalities. My eyes were gently opened in Ireland. I guess one might say that I gained an awareness, for the first time, of something that I had always known. We seem to have these doors within us that stay locked until somehow, somewhere, we find that little key. In Ireland I relearned the value of SIMPLICITY. I can't tell you about it yet, and my guess is that I may not be able tell you about it later. My best shot will be in the showing of it to you.

I was taught by people who don't teach. They had no plan, they had no intent, they had no motivation, and they had no idea. Their lives were the lesson.

This book isn't necessarily intended for Irish eyes. When I was asked to do this project, my first request was that only an "outsider" edit the photo selection. I want the illusion, of my personal experience of Ireland, to survive just a bit longer. The Irish are proud of an Ireland on the move — a European Community showplace. The tourist, on the other hand, strains to take in those fleeting pockets, and places, of an Ireland that once was. Thatched cottages sit abandoned. The dairies are automated. The back road traffic is now mostly made up of cars and buses. The B & B's are dry, spotless, warm and wonderful (the beds are even firm) and most accommodations have a private entrance. This, on the surface, is good news, but it doesn't come without a price. It is currently rare that travelers will have a chance to warm their hands over a peat fire, as they pass the time of day with family members. Do I long for a quaint little Ireland to live in, or just to visit? I'm happy that, in my writing, I don't have to answer the tough questions. I experienced the wonder of this place, and I have this rare opportunity to just cherish that memory. I hope you enjoy.

i turned up the lane. The dairy barn, in the rear, fit the description. Yes, this must be the Whelan place OK. I pulled up in front of a very typical Kerry farm house. And for the very first time I asked myself the question, "What am I doing here?" These people don't know me, and if I knock on the door, what am I going to say? If I can't explain it to myself, how do I make them understand what I'm after...what am I after? Maybe I ought to leave. Where would I go — back to California? No, I can't do that, what would I say to Nancy. I was muttering to myself, as I headed for the front door... "Her name is Kathleen (Karen told me that)...what if she asks me what I'm doing here...maybe nobody will be home." This became my only hope as I began to knock.

Maybe I ought to back up some. The events leading up to my squirming are segmented, and can only be described by sequencing a number of unconnected events, over a period of years. I guess the best place to start is at the beginning.

5

My brother Tom married Karen Whelan. She had just graduated from the University of California at Berkeley. Tom had finished law school, and while waiting for the results of his Bar exam, the young couple decided to backpack in Europe for the better part of the summer. They traveled far and wide, and Nancy and I joined them for a brief time in southern Spain. Upon their return, we all sat around for a long evening of "Show & Tell." "Click" they journeyed here, and "click" the show continued elsewhere. While attempting to connect with some of Karen's long lost relatives in Ireland, the face of a ruddy faced dairy farmer came up on the screen. I found myself strangely taken by the look of this man. The image disappeared, and I yelled to Tom, "Who was that man again?" Karen responded, "His name is Stephen Whelan, he is related to my dad's grandfather's side of the family." I don't recollect another slide from that evening, but I do visualize that face as if it were yesterday. I remember thinking, "Stephen Whelan...I'd very much like to meet him some day." End of story...or at least the end of that story.

Many years later things were happening in my life. I had an opportunity to travel on business to Japan. The Yen was 360 to one U.S. Dollar. It was pretty much required that all tourists buy both a wrist watch and a camera. I arrived home with my purchases. Digital watches for almost every member of our families, and a 35MM camera for myself. The latter seemed to take on a life of its own. Soon I would be converting a closet to a darkroom, and I found myself committing most of my free time to carrying this little device around. To make the longer story shorter, I attended a Jay Maisel photographic weekend workshop at the Mendocino Art Center on the California coast. It was very intense, and during the drive home I mentioned to Nancy that I wanted to do what he does. She responded, "Why don't you." Silently the wheels started to spin, and I began the long process of selling my retail store, and planning (later building) a studio. Add three years, and things were finally falling into place, other than I didn't really have a body of work to show any potential buyer of my photography. Plans were made, and plane tickets purchased, for a self assigned project of photographing the Alaskan King Crab fishermen on Kodiak Island. Nancy was still working, and I would travel alone.

I was sitting at my brand new desk, finalizing plans for the trip to Alaska, when it came over me. I must go to Ireland. I must go to Ireland now.

People who know me would generally agree that I'm not overly impulsive. Maybe to a fault, I'm a thinker, planner and executor type. Anyway, I picked up the phone and ask my travel agent to cancel my flight to Kodiak, and then confidently continued, "Book me the first available flight to Shannon." I put the phone down just as Nancy pulled into the driveway. It was noon. Over a sandwich, I said, "Oh, by the way...I'm on my way to Ireland."

Let's see, isn't this where we started? I did ask my sister-in-law to write to her Irish relatives. When I realized that there wouldn't be enough time, I then asked if she would give them a call. She tried, but never made a connection. Well, that was OK with me, because I hadn't made any connection between the Stephen Whelan image, that impressed me so many years before, and my plans (or lack thereof) for Ireland.

When I arrived at Shannon Airport, I rented a small car. I was more concerned about driving on the "wrong" side of the road than where I might be headed. I did have a map, and I found myself pointed in the direction of County Kerry. ✧

Chapter 2 Kathleen

The door opened. There, standing if front of me, was obviously the woman of the house. I asked, "Is this the Whelan residence?" She said, "It t'was." It was my turn again, and I asked, "Are you Kathleen?" When she nodded affirmatively, I then launched into a convoluted conversation that I couldn't bring myself to end. I told her my name, I mentioned my sister-in-law's maiden name, it went from there to trips, slides, Alaska, the weather, photography, and I might have mentioned how green I thought Ireland was...and then I took a breath. I always do that at the end of a sentence. She seemingly didn't respond to anything I was jabbering about. She did beckon me to come in, and then gestured for me to sit at a large circular table with an oil cloth. I was overcome by some necessity to explain myself, and I simply couldn't keep by mouth shut long enough to allow her any kind of a response that I could measure. It looked like she was preparing food, and I privately pondered the thought that her preparing food was better than her calling the police.

In a matter of minutes I found myself sitting in front of an Irish feast. By that time I was too rattled to be hungry. If I had indicated I didn't want to eat, she then might ask what I did want. I ate.

Only with my mouth full was she able to offer that she remembered Tom and Karen. I was relieved to at least have this connection established. She never asked then, nor later, about the WHY of my unexpected visit. Further more she didn't care. I came to her door, and that was enough. Little did I know that my first Irish lesson had begun, and I had survived...(in this case) myself.

Chapter 3 *Stephen*

*t*he door opened, and there stood Stephen Whelan. A giant was towering before me. His more than 300-pound frame was not only big but tall. His most recent activity was quickly revealed by his well-worn, pungent-smelling barnyard boots. Kathleen broke my awe with an introduction and from this point on, the beginning had begun.

Stephen Whelan

I truthfully can't remember the process of how we got so well acquainted, and how we got so comfortable with each other. Kathleen called a neighbor just down the road, and I had a place to stay that night. This B & B was the extra bedroom (extra income) type. I shared facilities with the family. Breda's husband, and young family, became part of my neighborhood discovery delight. I stayed all over western Ireland, but my overnights, "in the neighborhood" would be the journey I had traveled to experience.

Stephen and I did together what he would have been doing alone. He seemed to make no special effort on my behalf. I'm going to guess that he had never used a camera. Not once did he suggest a special location I might visit. When I would return from my travels, he would always greet me with a bellowing "Hi Roan, didya get any snaps?" He would then ask if I could join him to do whatever. I remember once he was trying to load a very large pig into his compact family four-door sedan. I have never seen a car with more dents. Automobiles that survive destruction derbies, to compete again and again, can't hold a candle to this vehicle. The back seat was out, and the squeeze was on. Only when he opened the window to allow the hog's head out was there barely enough room. On the road our conversations would then become lively, and I'm not sure he even noticed the wild eyed stares he was receiving from other drivers. After the livestock auction, or any other activity for that matter, there was always time to head to the pub.

To pour a pint is a time consuming celebration. The Guinness tap pressure would create a big head. The bar keeper would continue to attack the foam with a well used stick, and this cycle would be ceremoniously repeated numerous times. Deep discussions could be started, but all eyes were fixed on the activity at hand. When the dark draft, brimming full, was carefully offered across the bar, it would then be appropriate to order a second round. Everyone could then relax — all things were finally well in hand.

As we headed for the pub, others would join us. When we entered the pub, Stephen seemed to know everyone. He would make a big point of introducing me around. I was soon to learn, that in the neighborhood, if you were a friend of Stephen, you were no longer a stranger. The word spread. Up and down the road, the personal little stories I heard still fill my heart. Stephen was somebody. I watched. I listened. I learned.

Killarney National Park

Muckross House

Muckross Abbey

Killarney National Park

Kenmare

Chapter 4 *The Priest's Sister*

Maybe a little story, about a bigger feeling, might be fun. My Northern California home, and next door office, sit across from a rural Catholic church. My religion is rather undefined, and nondenominational, but I have enjoyed knowing a number of my good Irish priest neighbors. In the short time I had, between making my plane reservation, and actually boarding the flight, I was just scurrying around getting ready. It was after dark when I heard a quiet little knock. Upon opening the door I found Father Lenehan standing there with a worried expression on his face. I invited him in, and he immediately carried on about having just learned that I was on my way to Ireland, and that he wanted me to know that if I were to run into trouble over there, that he had relatives who could help. He started fishing around in his wallet for names, addresses and phone numbers. I told him that I appreciated his kind gesture, but that I would be fine, and he shouldn't worry...but he was firm in his concern. I took the little scraps of paper, and buried them in my wallet.

During my travels I began to make arrangements to arrive at B & Bs later in the evening. The reason for this is that the rate for an overnight stay is determined per person, and not per room. If I arrived in the early afternoon, I soon understood the dilemma I caused. If two people (say a couple) arrived later than I and wanted the room...well, anyway you get the idea.

I had stopped for some pub grub after a long day on the road. It was later than usual and darkness had set in when I headed down the road looking for some place to spend the night. That day, like many, had been spent simply wondering and wandering. I had absolutely no idea where I was, nor did I care for that matter. Finding interesting places to stay was surprisingly easy, but tonight, just a bed would do fine. I pulled up at the next B & B sign. An attractive young woman, twenty-ish, answered the door. It had taken a while to respond, and then she had no idea if any rooms were available. Away she flew up the stairs. She rushed back down to offer an out of breath, "Yes."

I was settled in when there was a knock at the door. Did I want a spot of tea? She brought the tea, and more (always more), and then expressed an interest in my nationality. I live in a very small farming community, and rather than add my town name of "Gridley," it has always proved easier just to respond, "California." She was a student at Trinity College in Dublin, and was home on holiday. I appreciated our little chat, and it was a nice way to end another delightful day in Ireland.

At breakfast the next morning, the girl's mother expressed an interest in my being from California. She asked, "Where aboot, in California, airye from?" I did my normal, and responded, "Northern California." After serving another couple, she returned to ask, "Where aboots, in Northern California?" After a short hesitation, I offered, "The Sacramento Valley." The pitch and volume of her voice elevated, "DOES IT HAVE A NAME?!" When I said Gridley, her face lit up, and it became obvious that her Irish breakfast chores would have to wait until she told me about her brother...the priest. I reached for my wallet, as she was carrying on. I looked up, and asked if her name was Ena Briggs? Her mouth dropped open, and it was a lot of fun exchanging tales from the coincidence. It was equally fun telling Father Lenehan later.

I got in my car and grabbed my wallet again. Hmmm, that means I must be in Mt. Bellew. Now that I knew where I was, I had to resort to a map to determine exactly where "where I was" was.

Dingle

Dingle Peninsula

Slea Head

24

Chapter 5 *From My Notes*

*M*ost of my travel work, in and out of the U.S., tends to be rural. I find that the little cultural differences are the ones that delight the most, and, more often than not, it is the every day event that tends to dominate my later fond memory. And, of course I love an Irish accent..."Ah yes Roan, meek noo mistake aboot it." And then there was that business sign, "Undertaker, Furniture, Manures?"

I spent considerable time just roaming the least traveled roads of Ireland. The road signs would start out Gaelic/English, and then peter out to Gaelic only. I became hopelessly lost one afternoon. I not only couldn't find my way, but I had lost all sense of direction in a very soft day. I finally came across an older couple working alongside their very modest cottage-type house. Using a map (holding it this way and then that way), add to that a lot of pointing here and then pointing there, and (all three of us) came up looking blankly at each other. It took some time, but we finally established that they knew where they were, but where I was (?)...was very much another matter. I thanked them and continued on. Later I went into a pub for directions, and my intended route immediately became a point of some intense discussion among the barman and patrons (the regulars) alike. Everyone kind'a joined in, and everyone seemed to have something significant to add. It was at least "a jar" later, when one chap summed it up as well as I think it could be told, "If I were headed there, I wouldn't be startin from here."

The joining of friends, neighbors and strangers, in business dealings, is another matter, and in sharp contrast to the ways of Americans — at least in California, where everyone seems to "secretly" negotiate deals in private. In Ireland, I couldn't bring myself to simply drive by an outdoor sheep (or cattle) fair, auction or market. Kenmare is normally a lovely small town. In late August (or was it early Sept.?) they hold a sheep fair in the middle of the town. Make-shift holding pens are set up in front of the shops. When buyers and sellers join, it becomes serious stuff, no matter what the nationality. What is so unique about this particular Irish experience is the number of "wandering by" outsiders who willingly volunteer a point of view. When a deal begins to show potential, eventually to be consummated with a hand slap, the gathering of folks begins in earnest. Sometimes the whole transactional entourage moves to a pub. Other times the buyer might start a walk-away process, that may turn into a drive-away "stop/start" routine. Then if negotiations get back on track, the vehicle gets left in the middle of the street. I've seen bystanders get so caught up in the action that they physically try to force the hands together. The tolerance level of the principles is nothing short of incredible, and it all remains very open and visual.

I can't leave my notes without mentioning a County Clare horse race near Lisdoonvarna. We start with a farmer's wet green cow pasture. A committee arrives early, but not too early, with stakes and a rope. Now we have a track. The race horses arrive via trailers, pulled mostly by small Japanese cars. The first one arrived, and it pulled into the pasture and promptly got stuck. Another followed, and it also went up to its axles. And then a third and a fourth, and so on. Everyone merrily got buried where they seemed contented to park. What appeared (in my very narrow mind set) as a giant bogged down mess seemed to concern no one else. The jockeys were very young boys. Now it's time for the crowd, vendors and turf accountants (book makers). Of course it starts to rain again, and the pasture/course eventually turns into a total mud bath. Neither the weather, nor the condition of the make-shift track had anything to do with anything. Everyone seemed to enjoy themselves. I did. Oh yeah, the race horses pull double duty — they also helped pulled the vehicles out of the mud. ∾

Traffic Jam

Lisdoonvarna

Aran Islands

38

Blennerville Windmill

Ballybunion

Chapter 6 Only 2 weeks?
An Irish Travel Itinerary

By Nancy Sanford

*i*f you only have two weeks to visit Ireland then I suggest that you concentrate your efforts in the west. Ireland is not a large island (300 miles long by 150 miles wide). An ambitious traveler can rush to most of the high spots, or can focus on less to experience more. I have found that nowhere in Ireland will you find the essence of the Irish expressed more warmly than in the west.

This itinerary is a slow paced adventure which allows the visitor time to walk through the countryside, take part in a local festival, join an impromptu session at an Irish pub, admire stunning historical reminders of Ireland's past and to just be available to a welcoming people.

Your port of disembarkation will be Shannon Airport in County Clare. From there a leisurely trip to Killarney will give you your first glimpse of the Irish countryside as you discover the countless shades of green woven into the fabric of the land. Killarney is a fun town of approximately 9,000 inhabitants, and planning a four day stay here will allow you time to un-jetlag, browse the many attractive shops featuring Irish handicrafts and enjoy day visits to the many attractions of County Kerry. Visits to the Lakes of Killarney National Park area and the Ring of Kerry are a must. Visiting the nearby village of Kenmare, during one of their sheep fairs, will give you a genuine feel for the Irish farmers' lifestyle. If you are inclined to the metropolitan then do make a visit to Tralee. Should you chance to be there in early September, be sure to take part in Ireland's largest festival, the International Rose of Tralee. An evening in Tralee is well spent attending a performance of the National Folk Theater of Ireland in the attractive Siamsa Tire Theatre. Your four days in the Killarney area should find you rested, relaxed and acclimated (be sure to bring your mist wear). Our journey continues north on to the Dingle Peninsula.

The Dingle Peninsula, a Fior-Ghaeltach (Irish speaking) district, is an enchanting region blending rolling green hills, golden beaches and a wild natural beauty. The peninsula's 160km can be covered in a single day but because of the spontaneity of our itinerary we chose to overnight at a delightful farmhouse B & B near the charming fishing village of Dingle. The peninsula, itself, is extremely rich in historical sites and antiquities dating to prehistoric times.

Of special note is the Gallarus Oratory, a fine example of early Irish dry rubble masonry, probably dating from the 8th century A.D. And no more spectacular scenery can be seen anywhere in Ireland than at the western most reaches of the peninsula called Slea Head. Perhaps you will recall the area from the David Lean film, Ryan's Daughter which was filmed there. The peninsula lends itself particularly to walking and there are a number of scenic and interesting trails throughout the area. Back on the road, our itinerary takes us still farther north, across the River Shannon, via car ferry, into County Clare.

County Clare lies at nearly mid-point on the Island's western seaboard. It is a diverse region with sweeping ocean views, the famous Cliffs of Moher, numerous lakes, and the also famous Burren, a unique region of karst (limestone with underground drainage). First we will visit the majestic Cliffs of Moher with ample time for a walk along its lofty (600') border. Our next stop along the Atlantic coast is the fishing village of Doolin. In recent years, Doolin has become known as "The Music Capital" of western Ireland, famous for its wealth of Irish folk music. Stopping at a pub here is the best way to tap into this Irish tradition. From Doolin we travel inland toward the famous Burren region of County Clare. At the crest of Corkscrew Hill we look down into Galway Bay and the fishing village of Ballyvaughan. We have cho-

sen to overnight here. From Ballyvaughan we will visit Lisdoonvarna where the local match-making festival might be in progress. Horse racing, while popular throughout Ireland, has special flavor as part of the festival's events. Here participants, spectators, and odds takers all gather in a local farmer's field where an impromptu track has been laid out in a muddy pasture. It's a wild ride, best described in Chapter 5. Also from Ballyvaughan it is a short distance to Kilfenora and its Burren Display Center. The center contains much information concerning the various aspects of the region: flora, fauna, geology, etc. Nearby are the Aillwee Caves where we have an opportunity to visit the Burren from underground. The access building is an architectural masterpiece and has won numerous awards for its designers. Any trip to the Burren would not be complete without a visit to the Poulnabrone Dolmen. This magnificent megalithic tomb dates from about 2,500 B.C. and is a fine example of Ireland's wealth of prehistoric monuments. Finally, a visit to the village of Kinvara will wind up our tour of County Clare. Kinvara is a charming market and fishing village on Galway Bay. A stroll through town found us admiring the work of a thatcher who was repairing the roof of one of the older cottages. Thatching is a dying art, we are informed, as synthetic materials replace traditional ones. Further on, at the edge of town, and by the seashore, stands Dunguaire Castle. Built in 1520 the castle is open to public view by day and hosts medieval banquets by night. On to County Galway—a region famous for its oysters and Oyster Festival.

County Galway is Ireland's second largest county. Today we will make a leisurely journey around Galway Bay. Our first stop is in the village of Clarinbridge for two reasons: a visit to the Clarinbridge Crystal showroom and a stop at the world famous Paddy Burke's Oyster Tavern for oysters and maybe a generous pint of Guinness to wash them down. Further along Galway Bay we encounter the City of Galway. This ancient city of the tribes has a recorded history of nearly 1,000 years. Today it is a bustling metropolis with a university, regional college, cathedral, shops, hotels, theaters, busy port and thriving industries. Here you will find the famous Eyre Square which is landscaped as a memorial garden to former U.S. President John F. Kennedy. While Galway offers a host of overnight accommodations, ranging from luxury hotels to cozy B & Bs, we are going to seek out the small village of Spiddal for our overnight. The main reason being that this is Sunday and on Sunday night Spiddal's only two pubs burst with activity and crowds of local merrymakers. The walls vibrate with Irish folk music and every visitor is encouraged to join in and is made to feel right at home. The atmosphere here brings to mind this quote, "In Ireland there are no strangers, only friends you haven't yet met." Following this evening of fun and frolic the morrow will find us en route to the Aran Islands.

We board our ferry at Roosaveal and a half hour later arrive at the dock in Kilronan, on Inishmore Island, the largest of the three islands. You are free to walk, bike or engage a horse and trap to sightsee the island. You are not permitted to bring a motor driven vehicle to the islands, however a few islanders own them. Here you will find that most residents embrace a traditional way of life. And, while this is an Irish speaking region, knowledge of English is widespread. The Aran Islands stretch 18 miles across the mouth of Galway Bay and consist mainly of limestone karsts presenting a stark nearly treeless landscape. There is scenic beauty in this starkness with sweeping vistas and massive cliffs to awe you. Historically noteworthy and well worth the short hike is the prehistoric monument of Dun Aengus. Our two days and nights here were most rewarding.

Our next stop in County Galway is the region known as Connemara. We will base our visit in the delightful village of Clifden, perched high above an inlet of Ardbear Bay. A walk along the Sky Road, with open vistas of the Atlantic Ocean, is a special treat for visitors. A favorite day trip into the region is to the beautiful Kylemore Abbey and Lake. Surrounded by mountains and nestled close to the Atlantic coast, Clifden is one of the most scenic villages in all of Ireland and is a favorite of mine.

The final night of our two week adventure will be at an accommodation near Bunratty Castle, conveniently located near Shannon Airport. Here you can enjoy a leisurely stroll through the Bunratty folk village where you will glimpse the traditional lifestyle of the Shannon region. Or perhaps you will choose to visit Bunratty Castle, a restored example of a Norman-Irish castle keep, originally built in the 1400s. Located on the grounds of the folk village, the castle features medieval banquets on a year round basis. In addition to traditional food and drink, the evening is filled with beautiful music and pageantry of the era. If, however, during your visit you have developed a passion for Ireland's national drink, that dense, dark stout which is dispensed with such precision, then a trip to Durty Nelly's is just for you. Durty Nelly's, located near the folk village, is filled nightly with the boisterous laughter and camaraderie of patrons about to depart this unique island. Your final stop on Irish soil is Shannon Airport. Here at Shannon's world famous duty-free shop is your last chance to stock up on all the souvenirs, crafts, whiskeys, etc., that Irish punts can buy. Loaded down with pleasant memories and infused with the warmth of the west, you will depart this Emerald Isle content to have had two unforgettable weeks and with a resolve to return for more.

Aran Islands

48

Doolin

Connemara

Clifden

Tory Sound
Co. Donegal

The Giant's Causeway

Dunluce Castle

Co. Antrim

Prehistoric Megalithic Tomb

Poulnabrone Dolmen

Co. Clare

Chapter 7 *Fly By Night Travel*

*i*n 1989 we brought our first group to Ireland. By this time Nancy had traveled extensively with me throughout all of the island. We decided on a travel itinerary that was to be both coastal and rural (she details our carefully selected route on page 42). Allow me here only to describe our beginnings, our first ever overseas attempt to share with others.

We had made prior overnight arrangements with guest inns, farmhouses, and other family-run B & B type accommodations. The group was made up of fifteen fellow travelers, and most nights would have us scattered among two or three neighboring locations. We felt the idea had merit, but that it would required a very special bus driver. I wanted the days to be sponta-neous and the evenings to be open. Our driver would, as a minimum, need to be both tolerant and flexible. We billed the trip as BUMP ALONG IRE-LAND, and my very best morning response to the question "What are we going to do today?" was, "I don't know."

We chartered a thirty-passenger bus that had the height of a regular coach, but was only half as long. This was to be our only luxury. We had a toilet, we had lots of room to spread out, we could get on and off in a hurry, and we could see over the fuscia hedgerows that seem to line every rural route. It was a near perfect system to do what we wanted it to do, but then there was our most memorable beginning....

We had plotted, we had planned, we wrote, we responded, we compared, and we finally had all our ducks lined up in a row. Never had we led a group out of the U.S., and we were extra careful about every little detail. The first leg of our flight (San Francisco to New York) got hung up for five hours at JFK. We final-ly took off across the Atlantic and touched down at Shannon mid-day. The group was wearily huddled in the middle of the airport while Nancy and I went looking for our bus. This coach was busy loading, that bus was just pulling away, and then I'd run over to another, only to be disappointed again. The few drivers remaining all seemed to know of the company we had chartered, but all agreed that there had been no such bus at anytime that day. It was Sunday, and we received no response from their office phone. In between, we'd check on the group. They gave us blank stares, too exhausted to complain.

Finally, someone at the airport was able to volunteer the name of the coach company's managing director or "boss". He lived in Dublin, and we caught him mowing his lawn. He then called Cork, and it was determined that they had the right date officially recorded, but wrong day marked on the calendar. It would be hours before all the necessary arrangements could be made. While still on the phone I happened to notice the local bus line pull up. I ran to the ticket counter and asked if they would eventually stop in Killarney. A "yes" to Killarney, and a "yes" to the question, "Can we purchase fifteen tickets?" was all it took. We boarded, and it was then fifteen bobbing heads all the way to our destination. The next morning someone dubbed our first travel accomplishment as something they might expect at FLY BY NIGHT TRAVEL. The name stuck.

Our bus eventually caught up with us that evening, and our driver was Kevin. Kevin truly made it happen. He loved our groups, and they loved him. He was a "can-do" driver, and (from the word go) we had the freedom to take advantage of all the unexpected delights that only seem to happen in independent travel. With Kevin at the wheel anything was possible — even if it was just a whim along the way.

When our second group arrived at Shannon Airport the next year we knew in advance that Kevin would again be our driver. Inside the airport we were greeted by Kevin's beaming face, and flying high above the waiting crowd was a large banner. It read "Fly By Night Travel."

n the first few chapters I've attempted to describe my first trip to Ireland. Even today I still wonder "how I got there," and I think often of Stephen. It was a strange impulse that seemed to drive me to change my plans, and go to Ireland. Clearly, I remember the sense of urgency that became part of my thinking. I've returned to Ireland a number of times since, but it is important now to finish the story I started.

My head was spinning during my first flight home. I, for the very first time, had experienced SIMPLICITY in its purest and most beautiful form. It had come to me less as a symbol and more as a directive. This idea still remains as a powerful force in my life, but, in practice, it can be illusive. I work at it. I succeed at it. I fail at it. I work at it some more.

Stephen was a rare human being. He never took me touring. He never offered to show me the sights. I stacked peat with him. I went to the market with him. I went to the pub with him. I drank Guinness with him. He sang me a goodbye song.

I arrived back in California. The first news I heard from Ireland was that Stephen had suffered a sudden heart attack. Stephen was dead.

I haven't got it fully figured out yet, but I'm learning to (or is it unlearning to?): trust chance, allow gifts given, accept the journey as enough, respect easy, and to keep the most important thing the most important thing. What a simple revelation it has become to recognize that the things I enjoy most are the things I do best. It's all so very simple, but then why does "simple" get so complicated? If I forget, and I frequently do, at least I know what I forgot. Thanks Stephen.